JESUS OUR LIFE

Faith and Life Series

BOOK TWO

Ignatius Press, San Francisco
Catholics United for the Faith, New Rochelle

Nihil Obstat: Rev. Msgr. Daniel V. Flynn, J.C.D.
                 Censor Librorum
Imprimatur: + Joseph T. O'Keefe
                 Vicar General, New York

Director: Rev. Msgr. Eugene Kevane, Ph.D.
Assistant Director and General Editor: Patricia I. Puccetti, M.A.
Writer: Daria M. Sockey
Artist : Gary Hoff
Photos : Gary Fuchs, Joe Rimkus, Jr. (N.C. News Service).

Catholics United for the Faith, Inc., and Ignatius Press gratefully acknowledge
the guidance and assistance of Reverend Monsignor Eugene Kevane, Director of
the Pontifical Catechetical Institute, Diocese of Arlington, Virginia, in the
production of this series. The series intends to implement the authentic approach
in Catholic catechesis given to the Church in the recent documents of the Holy
See and in particular the Conference of Joseph Cardinal Ratzinger on "Sources
and Transmission of Faith".

Excerpts from the revised edition of the Baltimore Catechism; copyright owned
by Confraternity of Christian Doctrine.

JESUS OUR LIFE

Contents

1   Our Heavenly Father

Do you know who God is? He is our Father in Heaven. He is great and holy. He loves you more than anyone else loves you.

God always wanted there to be someone just like you. So He made you. He gave you your hands and feet, your eyes and ears. God made you different from everyone else, because you are very special to Him.

God has also given you a soul. You cannot see your soul, but your soul is what makes you alive. If you did not have a soul, you could not think. You could not laugh. You could not talk. Your soul is what makes you do these things. Your soul gives you the power to do what is right and good. The soul is the part of you that never dies. It lives forever.

God our Father does not live only in Heaven. He is everywhere. He always sees you and watches over you. He always knows what you are doing and what you are thinking about. If you are ever alone or afraid, you should remember that God is with you and that He is your friend.

God wants you to be His child and to live someday with Him in Heaven.

One of God's great gifts to us is the Bible. The Bible is a big book. It tells us many things about God that we could not find out in any other way. God did not write the Bible. But He told the men who wrote it what to say. That is why we call the Bible the Word of God.

The Bible has two parts. The Old Testament tells how God made Heaven and Earth. It tells the story of the first sin. It tells us what people did for many years as they waited for the Savior.

The New Testament tells the story of Jesus: His birth, His life and teachings, and how He saved us from sin. It tells how the Church began.

At Mass on Sunday we hear three readings from the Bible.

Words to Know:

Heaven   soul   Bible   praise

"I will never forget you. See, upon the palms of My hands I have written your name."

(Isaiah 49:15—16)

Q. 1 *Who made you?*
God made me.

Q. 2 *Who is God?*
God is the all-perfect Being, Creator of Heaven and earth.

Q. 3 *Where is God?*
God is in Heaven, on earth, and in every place.

Q. 4 *Does God know everything?*
Yes, God knows everything, even our thoughts.

We Pray:

"I will give thanks to You, O Lord,
with all my heart;
in the presence of the angels
I will sing Your praise." *(Psalm 138)*

2   The Blessed Trinity

Once there was a time when there was no world. No earth, no sky, no people, no animals. There was nothing but God.

You may wonder, was God unhappy to be all alone? God did not need other things to make Him happy. And He was not really alone.

There is only one God, but in God there are three Persons. Their names are God the Father, God the Son, and God the Holy Spirit. The Father did not make the Son and the Spirit. The three Persons are equal and always were. All three are God. They are all-wise, all-powerful, and all-holy. We call the three Persons in one God the Blessed Trinity.

With the Son and the Spirit, God the Father created Heaven and earth. He made us and He made all things for us. He is the First Person of the Blessed Trinity.

God the Son is Jesus Christ. He is the Second Person of the Blessed Trinity. He came down from Heaven to be our Savior. He taught us all about God and showed us how to love Him. Jesus died for us and rose from the dead.

The Third Person of the Blessed Trinity is God the Holy Spirit. He helps us to pray, to be good, and to love God. The Holy Spirit comes to live in our souls when we are baptized.

It is hard to understand how God can be both three and one at the same time. Even very holy people don't understand it. So we say that the Blessed Trinity is a mystery. A mystery is something God wants us to know about, even if it is hard to understand. And if we love God, we want to know about Him, too!

Whenever we begin our prayers we make the Sign of the Cross. Every time we make the Sign of the Cross we are showing that we believe in the Trinity and the saving love of Jesus.

Words to Know:

Trinity   mystery

Praise God, from Whom all blessings flow;
Praise Him, all creatures here below;
Praise Him above, you heavenly host:
Praise Father, Son, and Holy Ghost.

Q. 5   *Is there only one God?*
Yes, there is only one God.

Q. 6   *How many Persons are there in God?*
In God there are three Persons—the
Father, the Son, and the Holy Spirit.

Q. 7   *What do we call the three Persons in one
God?*
We call the three Persons in one God
the Blessed Trinity.

We Pray:

Glory be to the Father, and to the Son, and to
the Holy Spirit, as it was in the beginning, is
now, and ever shall be, world without end.

Amen

3   God the Creator

God was happy all by Himself, but He wanted others to be happy too. So God made the world. Then God made people to enjoy all the wonderful things He made.

God made the world and everything in it. If we look at the sky, the ocean, or a mountain, we can learn how great God is. They are very big and powerful. Because God made them, we know He is even more powerful.

God made many beautiful things, too, like flowers, birds, sunsets, and rainbows. The beauty of these things comes from God.

We see that God is wise when we learn how He makes things grow and work together. He made great big trees come from tiny seeds. And each tree is a home for animals, birds, and bugs. God's plan takes care of everything He made.

God made all these things because He knew that we would like them. He made food that is good to eat and stars that are nice to look at. He even made things that make us laugh, like monkeys and puppies. God made them all because He loves us.

We can praise and thank God for His gifts by using them the right way. We should not waste our food. We should be kind to animals. We should keep the parks and forests clean when we visit them.

All things bright and beautiful,
All creatures great and small,
All things wise and wonderful,
The Lord God made them all.

Each little flower that opens, each little bird that sings,
He made their glowing colors, He made their tiny wings.

The purple-headed mountain, the river running by,
The sunset, and the morning that brightens up the sky.

The cold wind in the winter, the pleasant summer sun,
The ripe fruits in the garden, He made them every one.

He gave us eyes to see them, and lips that we might tell
How great is God Almighty, Who has made all things well.

Cecil Frances Alexander

Words to Know:

Creator

"And God saw everything that He had made and behold, it was very good."

(Genesis 1:31)

Q. 8 *Why is God called "the Creator of Heaven and earth?"*
God is called the Creator of Heaven and earth because He made it all out of nothing.

Q. 9 *Does God take care of all things?*
Yes, God takes care of all things.

We Pray:

Sun and moon, bless the Lord.
Stars of Heaven, bless the Lord.
Every shower and dew, bless the Lord.
All you winds, bless the Lord.
Mountains and hills, bless the Lord.
Everything growing from the earth, bless the Lord.
Seas and rivers, bless the Lord.
You dolphins and all water creatures, bless the Lord.
All you birds of the air, bless the Lord.
All you beasts, wild and tame, bless the Lord.

(Daniel 3)

4   God Made Us

God wanted to share the wonderful world He made, so He made the first man.

God gave him the name Adam. Adam lived in a beautiful place called the Garden of Eden. He was friends with all the animals, and he gave them their names. But soon God saw that Adam needed more than just the animals. God gave Adam someone who would love and help him. He made a good and beautiful woman. Her name was Eve.

Adam and Eve were very happy in the garden. They played with the animals and explored the woods and hills. They were never sick or hurt. They never felt like doing anything bad. They did not have to go to school, because God told them what they had to know. All the food they wanted was growing on the trees in the garden. Best of all, God would come to the garden to talk to them.

God loved Adam and Eve very much. He gave them a special gift called grace. Grace is a share in God's own life. With grace in their souls, Adam and Eve became God's children. Because of grace, Adam and Eve would someday be able to live with God in Heaven.

Later on, God made all the other people in the world; He made you. No two people look the same. Some of us are tall, others are short. Some of us have dark skin, others are light. There are boys and there are girls. God loves each of us just the way we are.

God wants us to know Him, to love Him, and to serve Him. He wants us to be His children and be happy with Him in Heaven.

"I will be a Father to you, and you will be My sons and daughters, says the Lord Almighty."

(2 Corinthians 6:18)

Words to Know:

grace   Adam and Eve   serve   guardian angel

> **Q. 10** *Why did God make you?*
> God made me to show His goodness and to make me happy with Him in Heaven.

Q. 11 *Who were the first man and woman?*
The first man and woman were Adam and Eve.

God has given each of us a guardian angel. Our angels protect us and help us to be good. You cannot see your angel, but he is always there. He follows you everywhere. You are never without your heavenly friend.

Learn this prayer to your guardian angel. Say it each day. Say it any time you feel lonely or afraid.

GUARDIAN ANGEL PRAYER

Angel of God, my guardian dear,
To whom God's love commits me here,
Ever this day be at my side,
To light and guard, to rule and guide. *Amen.*

5   God Is Offended

God also created the angels. Angels do not have bodies like us. They are spirits. Angels are much smarter and stronger than we are. We draw angels to look like people because they can think like us. We draw them with wings because angels can go anywhere as quickly as they wish to.

God made the angels to be happy with Him in Heaven and to be His helpers. But first He tested them to see if they loved Him. Some of the angels did not love God. They did not obey Him. They became devils. They were sent to Hell.

The good angels went to Heaven to praise God and to do His work on earth.

God also wanted to see if Adam and Eve loved Him. He gave them a test, too. He told Adam and Eve not to eat the fruit from one of the trees in the garden. They could have all they wanted from the other trees. God also said that if they ate from that one tree, it would make them very, very sad.

At first, Adam and Eve obeyed God. Then, one day Eve was alone in the garden. She met a snake. She did not know it, but it was really the devil.

"Eve," said the snake, "why don't you and Adam eat the fruit from this one tree?"

"God said not to," said Eve. "He said we would be very sad if we did."

"That is not true," said the snake. "If you eat this fruit you will be like God. You will know all things."

Eve should have known better than to think that God would lie to her. But she listened to the devil and ate the fruit. Then she told Adam, and he ate it too.

Because they disobeyed God, Adam and Eve had to leave the Garden of Eden. They had to work hard to get food to eat. The animals were now afraid of them.

Adam and Eve offended God. They sinned. Their sin took away the special gift of grace that God gave them. Without God's life in their souls, Adam and Eve could not please God. They could not go to Heaven.

We call this first sin of Adam and Eve *original sin*.

God still loved Adam and Eve even though they had sinned. So He promised to send someone who would save them and make it possible for them to go to Heaven someday.

"We will serve the Lord, our God, and obey His voice."

(Joshua 24:24)

Q. 12 *What are angels?*
Angels are created spirits without bodies.

Q. 13 *What is sin?*
Sin is disobedience to God's law.

Q. 14 *Who committed the first sin on earth?*
Our first parents, Adam and Eve, committed the first sin on earth.

Q. 15 *What is this sin called in us?*
This sin in us is called original sin.

Words to Know:

sin   original sin   offend   angel   devil   obey

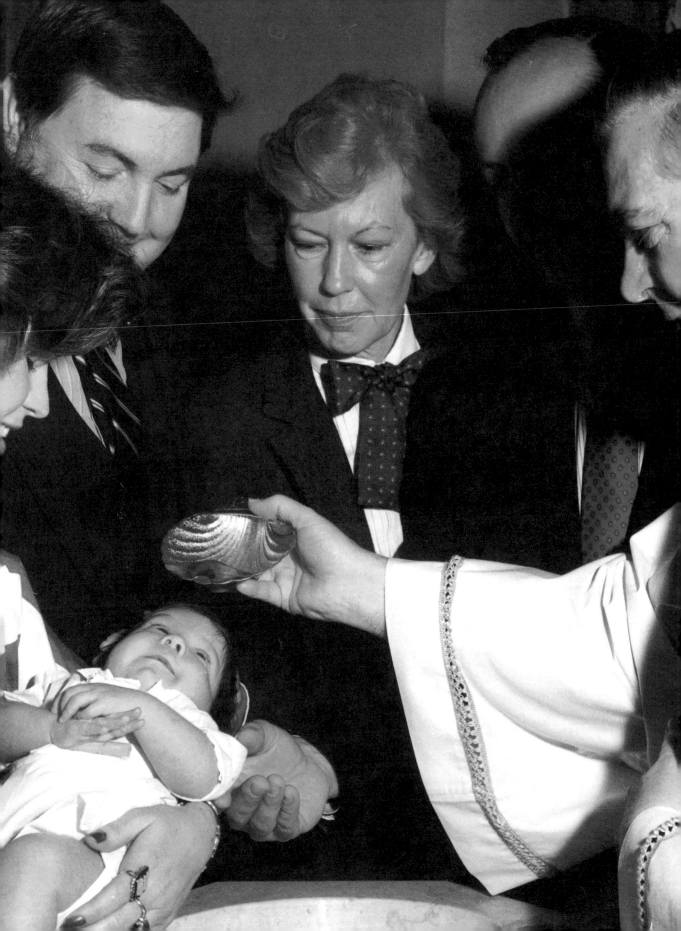

6 Becoming a Child of God

When Adam and Eve sinned, they lost the gift of God's life in their souls. They could not get to Heaven. Their children were born with original sin, too. They had no grace in their souls.

We call Adam and Eve our first parents because all people came from them. So do you. And we were all born with original sin on our souls.

At Baptism, original sin was washed away, and your soul was filled with God's life of grace. Now you are able to go to Heaven and be with God.

Baptism is like being born again. The first time we were born into the family of our mothers and fathers. At Baptism we are born into God's family, the Church. Then the Blessed Trinity comes to live in us.

We should try to keep our souls as clean and filled with grace as they were on the day of our Baptism. We should ask God to help us so we don't offend Him. If we keep God's life in our souls we will one day live with Him in Heaven.

What are some things we can do to keep our souls holy and pleasing to God?

First, we should pray. Thank God each day for making you His child. Talk to Him about the things that are on your mind because He is your friend.

Try to do the things God wants you to do. God wants you to love everyone. He wants you to obey your mother and father, even when you don't like what they tell you. God wants you to tell the truth.

Does that sound hard? Ask God and your guardian angel to help you to be good. And remember this: as long as you do no wrong, God wants you to have fun and enjoy the things He made for you!

Words to Know:

Baptism   sacrament

"I baptize you in the Name of the Father, and of the Son, and of the Holy Spirit."

(Words of Baptism)

Q. 16 *What is Baptism?*
Baptism is the sacrament that makes us Christians and members of the Church.

Q. 17 *What did Baptism do for you?*
Baptism washed away original sin from my soul and made it rich in the grace of God.

Every Catholic child is given a saint's name. It may be your first name, or it may be your middle name. A saint is someone who lives with God in Heaven. A saint is someone who loved God very much while on earth.

Ask your parents or teacher about the saint whose name you have. Maybe they know a story about him or her. Ask your saint to help *you* to be a saint someday too!

29

7 Obeying God Our Father

God still loved Adam and Eve, even after they disobeyed Him. He promised to send a Savior to make up for their sin and bring the Sacrament of Baptism. Then Adam, Eve, and all people would have the chance to go to Heaven.

But God did not say when the Savior would come. The people had to wait many years before Jesus came. Many people became tired of being good. They forgot about God. Soon there was only one family that still loved God. It was the family of Noah. You know the story about Noah and the ark. Noah obeyed God and made the ark even though everyone laughed at him. He wanted to do what God asked. Noah and his family stayed many days in the ark with the animals. They were not afraid of the flood because they knew God would keep them safe.

Years later there was a man named Abraham who loved God very much. But Abraham was sad because he didn't have any children. One day, God spoke to Abraham: "Your wife will have a baby soon. And someday you will have grandchildren, and great-grandchildren. Then the family of Abraham will be one of the biggest families of all!" God promised that the family of Abraham would always be very special to Him.

Soon Abraham's wife had a baby. She named him Isaac. Abraham loved his little boy more than anything else in the world.

One day, God tested Abraham. He told Abraham to give up his son. This made Abraham afraid and sad, but he wanted to obey God. When he was all ready to do what God had asked, an angel came and said, "Stop! You can keep Isaac with you. God just wanted to see how much you loved Him. God will bless you for being so obedient."

As God promised, the family of Abraham grew very large, and God took care of them all. Many of Abraham's descendants are living today. They are the people we call the Jews.

Many years after Abraham, but still long before Jesus came, there was a boy named David. David took care of his father's sheep all day. He was strong and good. He loved to sing and play a harp. He made up songs about God and the beautiful world God made.

One day, something happened that made all the

Jewish people very afraid. A giant named Goliath came and said he wanted to fight! "If you can find someone to beat me," he said, "my king will leave you alone. But if I beat you, you must all be the slaves of my king."

Everyone was afraid to fight Goliath. But not David. "I may be small, but God will help me to beat Goliath."

David took some small stones and put them in a slingshot. When he met Goliath in the field, the giant made fun of David. But David didn't care. He put a stone in the sling and shot Goliath right between the eyes. Goliath fell dead. David had saved his people.

Later, David became king of the chosen people. It was from his descendants that Mary and Joseph, the parents of Jesus, would come.

Words to Know:

Noah   Abraham   Isaac   David

8   God Gives Us His Laws

As God promised, the chosen people grew to be very many. Years after Abraham died, a bad thing happened to them. They all became slaves in the land of Egypt.

Then God gave the chosen people a leader. His name was Moses. With God's help Moses set the people free. For many years God led the people so they could find a new land to live in. God wanted His chosen people really to know that they were special to Him. He took care of them and showed His love for them by giving them all they needed. God also wanted them to love Him in return. He gave His chosen people rules and told them that if they loved Him they would obey those rules and they would be happy.

We call these rules the Ten Commandments. They are God's laws of love for all His people. Because we become God's children when we are baptized these laws are for us, too. Knowing God's laws helps us to do what is right.

Words to Know:

Ten Commandments   law

Here are the Ten Commandments:

1. You shall not have other gods beside Me.
2. You shall not use God's name in vain.
3. Remember to keep God's day holy.
4. Honor your father and mother.
5. You shall not kill.
6. You shall not commit adultery.
7. You shall not steal.
8. You shall not lie.
9. You shall not covet your neighbor's wife.
10. You shall not covet your neighbor's goods.

The first three Commandments tell us how to love and respect God. The others tell us how to love and respect other people. Sometimes we obey God's law by doing what is good, other times we obey by not doing what is bad.

"You are my friends if you do what I command you."

(John 14:15)

The Ten Commandments teach us:

It is right . . .	It is wrong . . .
— to pray to God.	— not to pray to God.
— to listen and pray in church.	— to misbehave in church.
— to use God's name with respect.	— to use God's name in the wrong way.
— to go to Mass on Sundays and holy days.	— to miss Mass on Sundays or holy days because of my own fault.
— to listen to and obey my parents and teachers.	— to disobey my parents and teachers.
— to be kind to everyone.	— to hurt others, to fight, or to be unkind.
— to be pure in my thoughts, words, and actions.	— to think and do bad things or say bad words.
— to be honest.	— to steal or cheat.
— to tell the truth.	— to lie.

9   I Choose to Love God

We learned that God the Father gave His people the Ten Commandments. Jesus gave us the Two Great Commandments. He told us that if we obey them, we would be obeying all the other Commandments at the same time.

The Two Great Commandments are:

1. *Love God with all your heart.*
2. *Love your neighbor as yourself.*

How do we love God? We love our Heavenly Father by praying to Him. Prayer means talking to God. We show our love by going to Mass on Sunday. At church we worship God with the other members of God's family. And we should talk about God with respect and love.

How do we love our neighbor? We love our neighbor by being kind and helpful to everyone we meet. We should love our parents and obey them cheerfully. We should share things with other children, and always tell the truth. We should pray for people who need God's help: the poor, the sick, people who are unhappy, and people who don't love God.

God gave you the power to choose to love Him. You can choose to do what you know is right or what you know is wrong. When you do wrong, it isn't because you "have to". No one "makes you" do it. Only you can choose. At times it is hard to be good, but that is when you show God that you really love Him.

If we do something bad on purpose, we commit a sin. We do not love God when we sin. Each sin that we commit takes grace away from our souls. Each sin turns us away from God. It is not a sin if we hurt someone by accident. It is not a sin if we forget to do something. But if we are tempted to do something wrong, and we think, "Yes, I will do it, even though I know it's wrong," then we commit a sin.

There are two kinds of sin. There are *venial* sins and *mortal* sins. Mortal sins are very big, very bad sins. Mortal sin kills the life of God in us. We cannot go to Heaven if there is a mortal sin on our souls. Venial sins are little sins, but they still make God sad. Most sins are venial sins.

It is sad but true that we all sin sometimes. Because of original sin we aren't always strong enough to say "no" to sin and "yes" to God. But God loves us very much and is always ready to forgive us.

"You, O Lord, are good and forgiving."

(Psalm 86:5)

Q. 18 *What is mortal sin?*
Mortal sin is a serious act of disobedience against the law of God.

Q. 19 *What is venial sin?*
Venial sin is a little act of disobedience against the law of God.

Every night think about the day you had. Did you do anything that was wrong? Are there times you did not do what was good? Look at the chart on page 37 to help you remember. Then tell God you are sorry. Ask Him to make you stronger next time. God will be glad to give you the grace to say "no" to sin.

Words to Know:

mortal sin   venial sin

41

10 Preparing for Our Savior

God wanted all of His people to be happy with Him forever. But because of Adam's sin, everyone lost the chance to go to Heaven. God promised Adam and Eve that He would send a Savior to make up for their sin and all the sins that were ever committed. The Savior would be Jesus Christ, God's own Son!

It was a long time before the Savior came. All that time, God spoke to His chosen people through holy men called prophets. Moses was a prophet. There were many others. They told people to stop sinning and to get ready for the coming of the Savior.

At last it was time for the Savior to come. God chose Mary to be His Mother. Mary was born without original sin. God made her that way. Mary's soul was always full of God's life. She was beautiful and good. Everyone liked to have Mary for a friend. Mary always did what God wanted her to do. She never said no to God and she kept all His commandments. She loved God very much and everyone else, too. God was very pleased by Mary.

One day God sent the angel Gabriel to Mary's house. He asked her to be the Mother of God's Son. She was surprised that God had picked her to be the Mother of the Savior, but she was happy, too. "Oh, yes," Mary said. "Let it be done to me as you say." Mary wanted to do whatever God asked of her.

God's people had to wait and get ready for many years before the Savior came. Each year, before Christmas, we spend time getting ready for Jesus too. We call this time Advent.

One way we prepare to celebrate the coming of Jesus is by making an Advent wreath. It is a wreath of evergreen branches with four candles—three purple candles and one pink one. Each candle stands for one of the four weeks in which we prepare for Christmas. We have Advent wreaths in our churches and in our homes.

Words to Know:

prophets   Gabriel   Mary   Advent

"Hail, full of grace, the Lord is with you!"

(Luke 1:28)

Q. 20 *Who is the Mother of Jesus?*
The Mother of Jesus is the Blessed Virgin Mary.

Q. 21 *Was anyone ever free from original sin?*
The Blessed Virgin Mary was free from original sin.

We Pray:

HAIL MARY

Hail Mary, full of grace!
The Lord is with thee.
Blessed art thou among women,
and blessed is the fruit of thy womb, Jesus.
Holy Mary, Mother of God,
pray for us sinners,
now and at the hour of our death. *Amen.*

11 The Savior Is Born

It was almost time for Mary's baby to be born when she and Joseph heard some news. The ruler of their land wanted to count all the people who lived there. Everyone had to travel to certain cities to be counted. Mary and Joseph had to go to Bethlehem.

When they got to Bethlehem, Mary and Joseph could not find a place to stay. So they had to stay in a stable with the animals. There, the baby Jesus was born. His bed was a manger filled with straw. This was part of God's plan. He did not want to come to earth as a rich king. He wanted to share the life of the poor.

That is why the first people to learn about the newborn Savior were poor shepherds. An angel came to them as they watched their sheep.

"I bring you good news," said the angel. "A Savior has been born to you. You will find Him lying in a manger." The shepherds hurried to find the newborn Savior. They found the baby Jesus with Mary and Joseph just as the angel had told them.

Far away, three wise men saw a big, bright star moving across the sky. They followed the star to see where it would take them. It led them to Jesus. The wise men gave precious gifts to the Savior, gifts you would give to a king. They knew that Jesus was a great king, even though He looked like a poor little baby.

A wicked man named Herod ruled over the land where Jesus was born. He met the wise men and heard them talk about a baby who was a king. Herod wanted no one to be king but himself. He was so angry he tried to have Jesus killed. But God warned Joseph to take Jesus and Mary far away so that Herod could not kill Jesus. They went to the land of Egypt, and there they lived until Herod was dead.

"The angel said to them: You have nothing to fear! I come to proclaim good news to you. . . . This day in David's city a Savior has been born to you, the Messiah and Lord."

(Luke 2:10−11)

Words to Know:

Christmas   Bethlehem   manger

48

Q. 22 *Where was Jesus born?*
Jesus Christ was born at Bethlehem, in a stable, and placed in a manger.

Q. 23 *When was Jesus born?*
Jesus was born on the first Christmas Day more than nineteen hundred years ago.

Q. 24 *Who is Jesus Christ?*
Jesus Christ is the Second Person of the Holy Trinity, true God and true man.

Q. 25 *Why did the Son of God become man?*
The Son of God became man to save us from our sins.

Away in the manger, no crib for a bed,
The little Lord Jesus laid down His sweet head;
The stars in the sky looked down where He lay,
The little Lord Jesus asleep on the hay.

Be near me, Lord Jesus, I ask You to stay,
Close by me forever, and love me, I pray;
Bless all the dear children in Your tender care,
And fit us for Heaven, to live with You there.

12 The Holy Family

After Herod died, it was safe for Jesus, Mary, and Joseph to leave Egypt. They went to live in a small town called Nazareth.

Joseph was the head of the Holy Family. He loved God very much and he loved Jesus and Mary too. Joseph worked hard all day so he could take care of Jesus and Mary. But he was always cheerful and kind. Joseph was a carpenter. He cut boards from trees and made them into tables and chairs. Jesus loved to watch Joseph at work. He was even happier when Joseph began teaching Him to be a carpenter.

Mary had a big job too. She took the money that Joseph made and went to buy the food the family needed. She baked bread, fixed meals, and made clothes for the three of them. Mary made the house a clean and happy place for Jesus and Joseph. Jesus also spent time helping His Mother around the house. He thought of ways to help her and to make her job easier.

Jesus loved to tell His parents all about the things He did and the games He played. He told them about

His friends and liked to bring them home. Mary and Joseph were glad that Jesus shared these things with them.

Jesus knew that His Heavenly Father wanted Him to do what Mary and Joseph told Him. So He always obeyed them, even when He wanted to do something else.

Jesus, Mary, and Joseph prayed together each day. They praised and thanked their Heavenly Father for His goodness.

Did you know that you and your family can belong to the Holy Family too? Jesus gave Mary to us to be our Mother. We can pray to St. Joseph as our friend and protector. And Jesus is our brother. Through Baptism He made us His brothers and sisters.

Words to Know:

Joseph   Nazareth   Holy Family

Q. 26 *Who is St. Joseph?*
St. Joseph is the foster-father of Jesus,
and Mary's husband.

Joseph most just . . .
Joseph most strong . . .
Joseph most obedient . . .
Joseph most faithful . . .
Head of the Holy Family . . .

Pray for us

We Pray:

God, our Heavenly Father,
help our family to be like
the Holy Family in Nazareth.

13   Good News

Jesus grew up and became a man. The time came for Him to leave the house in Nazareth and begin the work that God the Father sent Him to do. He said goodbye to His Mother Mary and started out.

First He went to the Jordan River to see John the Baptist. Jesus asked John to baptize Him. When John baptized Jesus the Spirit of God, looking like a dove, came to Him and God the Father spoke:

"This is my beloved Son, with Whom I am well pleased."

He said that so all the people would know that Jesus was the Son of God. Then Jesus went into the desert to pray.

After forty days, Jesus left the desert. He began to preach to people in towns and in the country. He told them that God loved them and wanted them to be with Him in Heaven. He said that God would soon save them from their sins. Jesus told lots of stories that made it easier to understand what God was like.

Jesus picked twelve young men to be His disciples. They would be His special helpers and would learn more from Jesus than the other people. The disciples soon learned from Jesus how to preach the Good News to others.

Jesus told many stories to teach us about the Kingdom of God.

The Mustard Seed

The Kingdom of God is like a mustard seed which someone plants in his field. The mustard seed is one of the smallest seeds but it grows into a very large plant. It grows so big that birds can build their nests in its branches.

The Buried Treasure

A man found a buried treasure in a field. He wanted to keep the treasure. But the field belonged to somebody else. So the man took all the money he had in the world. He bought the field so he could have the treasure.

When we learn the secret of how to live forever with God, it is like finding a buried treasure. When the man in the story bought the field, other people might have said, "Why is he spending so much money on an old field?" They did not know about the treasure. In the same way, some people do not understand why we follow God's laws. They do not know how wonderful Heaven is!

Jesus called everyone to live in the Kingdom of God. He taught us how to please God in our daily lives. He came to win us over to a life of friendship with God.

Words to Know:

John the Baptist   disciple
Good News   Kingdom of God

14   Jesus Our Teacher

One day Jesus told this story:

Once a man was travelling on a very dangerous road. It was a place where robbers would often wait to hurt people and take their belongings. And that is what happened to this man. He lay by the road, too hurt to move, and all his things had been stolen.

Soon a man came riding by. He saw the other man lying there, but he didn't care and rode on by. Another man did the same. Then a third man came, and he felt sorry for the man who had been robbed. He took the man to the next town, and he paid for the man to be taken care of.

This, said Jesus, is what it means to love your neighbor. It means to help those in need, and to be kind to everyone. Jesus said that if we do something kind for a person who needs our help, it is like doing it for Jesus Himself.

Here are some of the things Jesus said we should do, and some ways that we can do them:

Feed the Hungry and Give Drink to the Thirsty

Give money to the missions, bring food to your church Thanksgiving drive, help your mother fix dinner, eat the food you are given without complaining, as a sacrifice for the hungry.

Clothe the Naked

Send old clothing to the missions, lend your extra coat or gloves if your friend doesn't have his, help your little brother or sister to get dressed.

Shelter and Welcome the Homeless

If someone new moves to your neighborhood, make them feel welcome. Be a friend to the boy or girl in your class who seems lonely.

Visit and Comfort the Sick and Imprisoned

Go to see friends and neighbors when they are sick. If your classmate is sick, bring his schoolwork home and help him with it. Visit someone who is old and can't go out much; ask if you can help in any way.

Bury the Dead

We should pray every day for those who have died, even if we did not know them, so they will be happy in Heaven with God.

Words to Know:

Good Samaritan

15   Let Us Pray

The disciples knew that when they prayed they were talking to God, praising Him, and asking for what they needed. But they wanted to know how they should pray so they asked Jesus to teach them. Jesus taught them to say the prayer we call the "Our Father". By giving the disciples that one prayer Jesus was able to teach them how they should pray.

God wants us to call Him *Father*, because we are the children He loves. *Hallowed be Thy Name* is our wish that everyone use God's holy name with honor and respect.

We want God's Kingdom to come because then everyone will be His children. *Thy will* means the plan God has for us. If we all did what God wanted, as the angels do in Heaven, then earth would be a very happy place for everyone.

When we ask God for our *daily bread* we are really asking for all the things we need. With these words we are also praying for people who are poor and hungry, for those who are sick or lonely. We ask for what our souls need too.

We beg God to forgive our sins. The words *as we forgive those* remind us that if we want God to forgive us, we should be ready to forgive those who have done wrong to us.

We end the Our Father by asking God to keep us strong when we are tempted to sin. God will help us fight and win over evil.

Jesus told us other things about prayer. He said we should pray always. We can talk to God any time, at home, in school, or at play.

Jesus told us that God will give us what we ask of Him if it is good for us. Sometimes we have to wait a long time before God answers our prayers, but we shouldn't be afraid to keep asking. Jesus once told a story of a man who went to his friend's house late at night. He banged on the door and called out that he needed some bread. Even though the friend didn't want to get up, he finally did, because the man kept asking.

God loves you more than the man loved his friend, Jesus said, so you know that God will answer your prayers.

"Ask and you shall receive;
seek and you shall find;
knock and it shall be
opened to you."

(Luke 11:9)

Q. 27 *What is prayer?*
Prayer is talking with God to adore
Him, to thank Him, and to ask Him for
what we need.

We Pray:

MORNING OFFERING

O my God, I offer You every thought
and word and act of today.
Please bless me, my God,
and make me good today.

16   We Believe

Jesus wanted people to believe that He was the promised Savior and the Son of God. To help them believe, Jesus worked many miracles. By working these miracles He showed that He could do all things. Jesus is God, just as His Father is God.

The first miracle Jesus worked was at a wedding party. They had run out of wine to drink. Mary, Jesus' Mother, asked Him to help. Jesus took some water and changed it into wine.

Another time, Jesus and the disciples were in a boat on a lake. The wind started blowing hard. Soon big waves were crashing into the boat. The disciples were afraid. They woke up Jesus, Who was sleeping down inside the boat. "Lord, save us! The boat will sink!" Jesus got up and said "Be still" to the wind and water. At once the storm ended. The disciples were so surprised to see the wind obey Jesus.

One day Jesus was teaching a great big crowd all day. He felt sorry for them because they didn't have anything to eat so he told the disciples to feed the people. The disciples told Jesus, "We have only five loaves of bread and two fish. That will not feed five thousand people! And there are no stores nearby, either." Jesus took the bread and fish and, by blessing them, made them into enough food to feed all five thousand. There was so much food that twelve baskets of scraps were left over!

Most of the miracles of Jesus were to help people who were sick or hurt and to show that He loves them. He made blind people see again. If someone couldn't walk, Jesus said, "Get up," and he could walk again.

One day a man named Jairus came up to Jesus. "Please come to my house," he said. "My little girl is very sick. I'm afraid she will die. But if you come and lay your hands on her, I know she will get better."

Jesus went with Jairus. When they got to the house, everyone was crying. "It's too late," they said. "She is dead."

But the power of Jesus was stronger than death. He went inside and took the girl's hand. "Get up, little girl," He said, and with that she opened her eyes and got up, alive and well!

Words to Know:

miracles

"Yes, Lord, I have come to believe that you are the Messiah, the Son of God: He Who is to come into the world."

(John 11:27)

We Pray:

Jesus, I believe in You.
You are truly the Son of God.

17   Asking Forgiveness

Sometimes we break God's laws. We commit a sin. What happens then? What does God do, and what should we do?

Although God hates sin, He loves you very much. He is always ready to forgive you when you are sorry for the sins you committed. Jesus told this story to show how God loves and forgives.

There was once a rich farmer who had two sons. The younger son said, "Father, I know that someday when you die, my brother and I will get all your money. Well, I want my half right now." So the father gave him the money. The son ran away and spent the money unwisely. Soon he had wasted it all, and he was now poor and hungry. He found a job herding pigs, but he was still hungry and lonely. One day, he said, "I've been so bad that my father won't want me for his son anymore. But maybe I can get a job on his farm. At least that way, I'll be near my home."

The son was wrong. His father saw him coming. He was so happy that he did not care about how bad his son had been. The son said, "Father, I have sinned against Heaven and you. I am not good enough to be your son." But the father didn't even listen. He knew his son was sorry and was happy to have him back. He invited all his friends to a big party to celebrate his son's return.

Our Heavenly Father is just like the father in the story. Sometimes we sin and "run away" from God like the younger son. That makes us sad because when we sin we offend God Who loves us very much. But God wants us to be happy. He wants us to come back to Him. All we have to do is admit that what we have done is wrong. And then we must be truly sorry that we have offended God. God will be waiting for us with open arms.

God will always forgive us. There is nothing we can do that is so bad that God won't forgive if we are truly sorry. It shows God that we really love Him when we tell Him we are sorry for having offended Him and want to be forgiven.

Words to Know:

forgive   sorrow

Q. 28 *What is sorrow for sins?*
Being sorry for the sins we have committed and wanting never to commit them again.

We Pray:

ACT OF CONTRITION

O my God, I am heartily sorry for having offended You. I detest all my sins because of Your just punishments, but most of all because they offend You, my God, Who are all-good and deserving of all my love. I firmly resolve, with the help of Your grace, to confess my sins, to do penance, and to amend my life. *Amen.*

18   Jesus Forgives

There were many times when Jesus cured sick people. And there were also many times when He forgave their sins. Jesus is always ready to forgive us when we are sorry for having offended Him.

Only God can forgive sins. Jesus showed that He was God by curing people and forgiving their sins. Jesus made some of the disciples His first priests. He gave them special powers. One of these is the power to forgive sins. Priests today have this power too. God forgives our sins through them.

When God uses a priest to forgive our sins, it is called the Sacrament of Penance. It is also called Confession because we "confess", or tell, our sins to the priest.

The priest takes the place of Jesus. When we confess our sins it is Jesus Who hears us and Who forgives us.

Before we go to confess our sins, we must get ready. We should think about our sins and be sorry for them. Then we tell our sins to the priest. He forgives us by saying:

"I absolve you from your sins in the Name of the Father, and of the Son, and of the Holy Spirit. Amen."

The Sacrament of Penance does more than take our sins away. It gives us grace. Grace makes us closer to God and helps us to be stronger against sin.

The priest will never tell our sins to anyone. He only wants to bring us God's forgiveness. He wants to help us to be good.

Words to Know:

absolve   confess

"If you forgive men's sins they are forgiven them."

(John 20:23)

Q. 29 *What is the Sacrament of Penance?*
Penance is the sacrament by which sins committed after Baptism are forgiven.

We Pray:

Lord Jesus, You cured the sick and forgave sinners. Forgive me and keep me in Your love.

19   The Sacrament of Penance

When you are going to do something special, you have to get ready for it. If you are going away on a trip, you don't just get in the car and ride away. First you think about the things you want to take with you. Then you find the things and pack them.

You also have to get ready before you receive the Sacrament of Penance. First, you should ask God the Holy Spirit to help you remember your sins. Think about what you have done wrong, and how many times you did it.

Then, try to be sorry for your sins. Think of how your sins hurt Jesus. Make up your mind not to sin again. Say an Act of Contrition, which tells God that you are sorry.

After this, it is time to receive the Sacrament. The priest will welcome you. You then make the Sign of the Cross. The priest may then read to you from the Bible.

Next you say how long it has been since your last Confession. Then you tell the priest your sins. When you have finished, say, "For these and all my sins, I am sorry." The priest will talk to you and give you a penance.

A penance is what the priest tells you to do to help you make up for the wrong you have done to God, to others, and to yourself. Sometimes the penance may be to say a few prayers or to do something for someone.

The priest may then ask you to pray an Act of Contrition. After that, he will forgive you in the name of Jesus: "I absolve you from your sins in the name of the Father, and of the Son, and of the Holy Spirit." You will answer: "Amen."

The priest then says: "Give thanks to the Lord for He is good." Your answer is: "His mercy endures forever."

The Sacrament of Penance helps us to be strong and holy Christians. It keeps us in God's friendship.

Words to Know:

Sacrament of Penance

"May the Lord be in your heart and help you to confess your sins with true sorrow."

(Rite of Penance)

Steps for the Sacrament of Confession:

1. Know what my sins are.
2. Be sorry for my sins.
3. Make up my mind not to sin again.
4. Tell my sins to the priest.
5. Do the penance the priest gives me.

We Pray:

Give thanks to the Lord for He is good and His mercy endures forever.

20 Making Up For Our Offenses

One day, a big crowd of people was with Jesus. A little man named Zacchaeus went up in a tree so he could see. Jesus saw him and called out, "Zacchaeus, I would like to come to eat dinner at your house." Zacchaeus was happy, but also sad. He knew his sins offended Jesus. So Zacchaeus told Jesus he would make up for his sins. He paid people four times the money he had taken from them.

Jesus died for us to make up for our sins. We can make up for our sins, too.

Once a boy was playing in his house. He was throwing a ball around, even though his mother had said not to throw balls inside. The ball hit a beautiful vase and broke it. The boy told his mother what had happened. He said he was sorry and would never throw the ball inside again. "That's all right. I forgive you," said his mother.

But the boy wanted to make up for what he did. He picked up all the broken pieces. Then, instead of going to play, he went and picked some flowers. His mother looked so happy when he gave her the flowers. That made the boy feel glad.

How can you make up for your sins? First, you can do the penance the priest gives you when you go to Confession. Because you love God, you can do something more. You could not watch TV for one day and use that time to help your mother or father. You could play with your little brother or sister instead of your friends. It is hard to give up things you like, but it will make you strong. It will help you to say "no" to what is wrong.

Sometimes there is one sin that you commit more than others. It may be lying, or disobeying, or fighting with others. You should try hard to stop this bad habit, and to start a good habit. By going to confession often, you will have the grace to stay away from sin.

Remember: the reason why you want to make up for your sins is to please Jesus. If you think of that it will be easier to do something that is hard for you to do.

Can You Answer?

1. When does a person sin?
2. How do you know what is right or wrong?
3. Why should you be sorry for your sins?
4. Does God love you even when you sin?
5. What does it mean to be truly sorry?
6. Why do we go to Confession?
7. Who takes away your sins?
8. Whose place does the priest take in Confession?
9. What does the priest say to forgive you?
10. What must you do to make a good confession?
11. The priest gives you a penance. What is this penance for?
12. Besides being forgiven, what happens to you when you go to Confession?

21 The Good Shepherd

The time came when Jesus knew He would soon die for us. He rode on a donkey into the city of Jerusalem. Nobody else knew Jesus was going to die. Many people came to honor Jesus as king. They threw palm branches and coats onto the road where He was coming. They shouted for joy.

The people were right to think Jesus was King. But He was not the kind of king they wanted. Jesus is King of Heaven as well as earth. He did not come to live in a palace and wear a crown. He came to be the Savior Who would die for our sins and lead us to Heaven.

"I am the Good Shepherd," said Jesus. "I know my sheep and they know me. They hear my voice. I know them and they follow me."

We are the sheep that Jesus speaks of. Just like a shepherd, Jesus watches over us night and day. He knows all about each one of us. He knows everything we say and do. Jesus even knows what we want and what will make us happy.

A shepherd must feed his sheep. Jesus gives us food for our souls in the sacraments. This food makes us strong so we will be good.

A shepherd protects his sheep from the wolves and other dangers, and he finds those sheep that have gotten lost. Jesus guards us against evil and sin. But even when we turn away from Jesus by sinning, He will always come after us, calling us back to His love.

A shepherd leads his sheep to green pastures where they will be happy. Jesus came to lead all of us on the way to Heaven—the only place where we will be truly happy. He taught us that He is the Way and that we must become like Him to go to Heaven.

"The Good Shepherd lays down His life for His sheep." Jesus was brave enough to lay down His life for us. He died so that we all could live forever. Even if you were the only boy or girl in the world, Jesus would have died just for you. He loves you that much.

Words to Know:

Good Shepherd

"I am the Way, and the Truth, and the Life; no one comes to the Father but through Me."

(John 14:6)

Jesus Is the Way — We Must Become Like Him

obedient:	Always do what pleases God. Obey cheerfully.
humble:	Tell the truth. Never lie.
forgiving:	Love your enemies. Forgive those who hurt you.
prayerful:	Say your daily prayers. Always be mindful of God's presence.
merciful:	Be kind to everyone. Be helpful and generous.

We Pray:

Jesus, meek and humble of heart,
make our hearts like to Yours.

22   The Last Supper

Every year, the Jews had a great feast called Passover. This was to remember the time when God led Moses and the chosen people out of slavery.

The night before Jesus died, He celebrated the Passover dinner with His twelve disciples. Jesus felt very sad to be leaving His friends. He wanted there to be a way that He could always stay with them, and with all those who loved Him.

So while they were eating, Jesus took some bread. He prayed to His Father, blessed the bread, and broke it. He gave it to the disciples and said,

"This is My Body, which is being given up for you."

Then Jesus took a cup of wine and said,

"This is the cup of My Blood. . . . It will be shed for you so that sins may be forgiven."

With those words, the bread and wine became the Body and Blood of Jesus. It was not bread and wine anymore, but Jesus. When the disciples ate it, Jesus came to live in their souls. This was the first time anyone had received Holy Communion.

We call the Sacrament of Christ's Body and Blood the Holy Eucharist. At the Last Supper Jesus said to His disciples, "Do this in memory of me." At every Mass the priest says the words of Jesus, and so the bread and wine are changed into Jesus' Body and Blood.

Living Bread

Remember when Jesus fed the crowd of five thousand people with only five loaves of bread and two fish? The people were all amazed and wanted Jesus to do it for them again. But Jesus told them that He would give them food that would make them live forever. He told them that He was that living bread.

Jesus gave this living bread for the first time to His disciples at the Last Supper and He gives it to us in Holy Communion.

"I Myself am the living bread come down from Heaven. If anyone eats this bread he shall live forever; the bread I will give is My flesh, for the life of the world."

(John 6:51)

Q. 30 *What is the Eucharist?*
The Eucharist is the Sacrament of the real Body and Blood of our Lord, Jesus Christ.

Q. 31 *When did Jesus give us the Eucharist?*
Jesus gave us the Sacrament of the Eucharist at the Last Supper.

Words to Know:

Last Supper   Holy Eucharist   Communion

23   Jesus Dies for Us

After the Last Supper, Jesus and the disciples went to the Garden of Olives. He asked them to pray with Him, but they were tired and fell asleep. So, all by Himself, Jesus began to pray. He felt sad when He thought about our sins. Jesus asked His Father to make Him strong and brave. He told His Father, "I will do what You want."

Soldiers came to arrest Jesus. Pilate said that Jesus should die. The soldiers hit Jesus and beat Him with whips. They put a crown of thorns on His head and slapped Him, saying, "Hail, King of the Jews."

Jesus had to carry a heavy Cross through the streets. The weight of our sins made it even more heavy. Sometimes Jesus fell down.

At Mount Calvary Jesus was nailed to the Cross. Even then He did not stop loving everyone. He prayed for the people who wanted to kill Him, "Father, forgive them." He forgave the good thief. He gave His Mother, Mary, to be the Mother of all God's children.

Some people called out, "If you are the Son of God, come down from the Cross!" Because Jesus was God,

He could have done this. But He wanted to suffer and die because He loved us. And He wanted to obey His Heavenly Father.

Finally Jesus died. At that moment the gates of Heaven were opened. We were brought back to the friendship of God which Adam and Eve had lost.

Words to Know:

Cross   Passion   Calvary

Q. 32 *What did Jesus Christ do to save us?*
To save us, Jesus Christ made up for our sins by suffering and dying on the Cross.

We Pray:

We adore You, O Christ, and we bless You, because by Your Holy Cross You have redeemed the world.

96

Stations of the Cross

1. Jesus is condemned to death.
2. Jesus carries His Cross.
3. Jesus falls the first time.
4. Jesus meets His Mother.
5. Jesus is helped by Simon.
6. Veronica wipes the face of Jesus.
7. Jesus falls a second time.
8. Jesus speaks to the women.
9. Jesus falls a third time.
10. Jesus is stripped of His clothes.
11. Jesus is nailed to the Cross.
12. Jesus dies on the Cross.
13. Jesus is taken down from the Cross.
14. Jesus is placed in the tomb.

24   He Is Risen, Alleluia!

Early in the morning the Sunday after Jesus died, some women came to visit His tomb. All the way over they worried about the big stone that closed the tomb. "Who will roll it away for us?" they wondered.

But when they got there, the stone was already rolled back. A beautiful angel was sitting on it. "Why do you look in a tomb for someone who is alive?" he said. "Jesus is not here. He is risen. Go and tell the others."

Very surprised and a little afraid, the women ran off. The disciples did not believe them, even though Jesus used to tell them that He would die and rise again. But soon different friends of Jesus saw Him. Mary Magdalen and the other women saw Him first.

A few days later, the disciples were together in one room. The door was locked. All at once Jesus was there with them! "Peace be with you," He said. He talked and ate with them so they could see it was not a ghost, but really Jesus. How happy the disciples were! Jesus was alive again.

"Peace be with you." The disciples no longer felt any fear or sadness when Jesus was with them. We, too, will have peace when we let Jesus come into our lives.

That is why Easter is such a joyful time. We celebrate because Jesus is alive and has won for us the life of grace. Now we can live forever!

Q. 33 *After His death, what did Jesus Christ do?*
After His death He rose from the dead.

Words to Know:

Easter   Resurrection

Jesus Christ is risen today, alleluia,
Our triumphant holy day, alleluia,
Who did once upon the Cross, alleluia,
Suffer to redeem our loss, alleluia.

Hymns of praise then let us sing, alleluia,
Unto Christ our Heavenly King, alleluia,
Who endured the Cross and grave, alleluia,
Sinners to redeem and save, alleluia.

On Easter Sunday there is a special candle in the church. It is called a Paschal Candle. We light it on Easter to remind us of Jesus' Resurrection.

Sometimes we call Jesus the Light of the World. The Paschal Candle is a symbol for Jesus.

We Pray:

May the Light of Christ,
rising in glory,
dispel the darkness
of our hearts and minds.

25 The Holy Mass

Every Sunday we go to church to do what Jesus told the disciples to do when He said, "Do this in memory of Me." You see, the Last Supper was the very first Mass.

At the Last Supper, Jesus changed bread and wine into His Body and Blood. He gave the disciples the power to do this too. The disciples gave that power to other men. That is why our priest today can change bread and wine into the Body and Blood of Christ at every Mass.

At Mass we offer the same sacrifice that Jesus offered for our sins. That is the sacrifice which Jesus offered to the Father when He died on the Cross. A sacrifice is the total giving up of something. Jesus gave Himself up to God the Father for us. This is the sacrifice we offer at every Mass.

We also celebrate the Resurrection. That is why we go to Mass on Sunday, because Jesus rose from the dead on a Sunday. Each Sunday is a "little Easter". This is a community celebration and that is why we all come together on Sunday.

Why do we go to Holy Mass?

We go to praise our God, Who is great and good.

We go to say "thank you" to God for all the good things he has given us.

At Mass we tell God we are sorry for our sins, and we ask His help to be better.

We also pray for the things we need, and for the needs of others.

If we listen carefully to the Mass and try to say the prayers, God will give us His grace and blessing. Taking part in the Mass will help to prepare you for your First Communion.

Q. 34 *What is the Mass?*
The Mass is the sacrifice of Jesus on the Cross, offered in our church by the priest.

Q. 35 *Why is the Mass offered to God?*
The Mass is offered to God to worship Him, to thank Him, to make up for our sins, and to ask His help.

Sunday Is God's Day

The Third Commandment says: Remember to keep holy the Lord's Day. By going to Mass on Sunday we are obeying God's law and keeping His Day holy. But we should do more than just go to Mass on Sunday to honor God. We should make it a special day and we can do that by:

— not doing any work that can be done on another day.

— wearing our best clothes when we go to church.

— not going shopping.

— having a special meal with our family.

— spending time together with our family.

— spending more time thinking and talking about God.

Words to Know:

Mass   sacrifice

26   What We Do at Mass

The Mass has many parts leading up to the coming of Jesus in the Eucharist. They are like steps on a ladder that climbs up to Jesus.

We begin the Mass by singing a hymn or saying a prayer while the priest goes to the altar. Then we make the Sign of the Cross.

Next the priest asks us to think of the ways we have hurt God and others. We say the *I Confess* prayer which asks forgiveness. This prayer also asks Mary, the saints, and those in church to pray for us. Then comes a song of praise, *Glory to God*.

After this we sit down to hear the *Word of God*. The lector and the priest read to us from the Bible. We learn about God's chosen people, and about the life of Jesus. The priest gives a sermon to help us understand the Bible and lead good lives.

We stand to say the *Creed*. The Creed tells what we believe as Catholics. It tells what our parents promised we would believe at our Baptism.

At the *Offertory* the bread and wine is brought to the altar. We offer ourselves as a gift to God. Also, we give our money to help our church.

Then we kneel down, and the priest says a long prayer to prepare us for the *Holy Eucharist*. He says the words of Jesus:

"This is My Body."
"This is the cup of My Blood."

And the bread and wine become Jesus, our Savior.

After this we stand and say the *Our Father*, then give the sign of peace to one another. Then the people go to receive our Lord in *Holy Communion*. They kneel down and spend some time talking to Jesus, Who now lives in their souls.

The priest ends Mass with a *Blessing*, and says, "The Mass is ended. Go in peace." We leave the church, and we try to spend the rest of the day in a way that is pleasing to God.

Altar	The table Mass is offered on.
Chalice	The cup of precious material that holds the Blood of Jesus at Mass.
Ciborium	The cup of precious material that holds the Hosts people receive at Communion.
Cruets	The bottles that hold the water and wine.
Missal	The book with the prayers for Mass.
Paten	The plate of precious material that holds the Host, the Body of Jesus.

Parts Of The Mass	What The Priest Does	What We Do
Entrance:	goes to the altar gives greeting	sing a hymn or say opening prayer ask forgiveness for our sins
Readings:	reads from the Bible	listen to the Word of God
Offertory:	offers the bread and wine to God	offer ourselves to God
Consecration:	changes the bread and wine into the Body and Blood of Jesus	offer Jesus as sacrifice to the Father
Communion:	gives the people the Body and Blood of Jesus	receive the Body and Blood of Jesus
Blessing:	blesses and dismisses the people	receive God's blessing

27 Jesus Comes to Us

A very important part of the Mass is called the Consecration. This is when the priest takes the bread and wine and says:

"This is My Body."
"This is My Blood."

At that moment, Jesus is there on the altar. We should all adore Jesus. We can pray the words of St. Thomas, the apostle, when he met the risen Jesus:

"My Lord and My God."

By praying this, we are telling God that we really believe that Jesus is present.

When you receive Holy Communion, it will be one of the greatest things that ever happened to you. At Baptism you received a share in God's life. When you receive Holy Communion you will have even more of God's life. Jesus, Himself, will be with you.

Just as food makes our bodies grow, Holy Communion makes our souls strong and beautiful. Jesus will be closer to you than ever before. He will listen to everything you tell Him.

One day, when Jesus was out teaching, lots of children came to see Him. The disciples started to say, "No, boys and girls, don't bother Jesus now." Jesus told the disciples that they were wrong. "Let the children come to me, and don't stop them. The Kingdom of Heaven is for them." Then Jesus began talking and playing with the children. He put them on His lap and blessed them.

Jesus is waiting for you to come to Him. He wants very much to hold you close and bless you.

The Bread of Life

Holy Communion is food for our souls.

It gives us life — God's life and love.

It makes us grow — as children of God.

It keeps us healthy — by helping us do what is right.

When we eat this Bread and drink this Cup we proclaim Your death, Lord Jesus, until You come in glory.

(Words from Mass)

Q. 36 *When do the bread and wine become the Body and Blood of Jesus?*
The bread and wine become the Body and Blood of Jesus at the Consecration.

Words to Know:

Consecration

28 Jesus, My Lord
And My God

There are things we should do to get ready for our First Communion.

First, we must make sure our souls are healthy. We may never receive Holy Communion if we have a mortal sin on our souls. We must receive the Sacrament of Penance first. It is a good idea to go to Confession often even if we only have small sins. This will give us grace and make us strong enough to keep away from mortal sin.

We should try to show in our lives that we love Jesus. This means that we say our prayers morning and night, and that we obey our parents. It means being kind and loving to all those around us.

We also prepare to receive Jesus by not eating or drinking one hour before Holy Communion.

In church we get ready for Jesus by paying attention to the Mass and making the responses. During quiet times in the Mass, we can say our own prayers to Jesus. We can tell Him how glad we are that He will soon come to us.

We should walk up to receive Communion quietly. This is not the time to look around at the other people. It is time to think about Jesus. We should receive Jesus with love and respect.

When we get back to our seats we will kneel down and close our eyes. We can tell Jesus anything we want. He is glad to hear it all. We can ask Him to make us more like Him and to help us not to sin. We can ask Him to bless our family and friends.

Sometimes instead of talking to Jesus, it is nice to quietly enjoy having Jesus in our hearts. He does not need to hear lots of words from us. Just say "I love you, Jesus." That is what Jesus wants to hear most of all.

Q. 37 *What is necessary to receive Holy Communion?*
To receive Holy Communion you must be in the grace of God, believe it is Jesus you are going to receive, and fast for one hour before.

Before Holy Communion:

Think about Jesus and how much He loves you. Pray to Him telling Him that you:

— believe in Him.

— hope in Him.

— love Him.

— are sorry for ever offending Him.

— want Him to come to you.

After Holy Communion:

Pray to Jesus to:

— thank Him for coming to you.

— tell Him that you love Him and always want Him to be with you.

— ask Him to help you and other people.

29　Jesus Returns To the Father

After He rose from the dead, Jesus stayed here on earth for forty days. He appeared to His disciples many times. He gave the apostles the power to forgive sins. He told them how to bring the Good News to places all over the world. Apostle means one "who is sent". Jesus was sending them to teach all people about His saving love.

One day, the apostles were out in a boat, fishing. They could not find many fish. A voice from the shore called, "Throw your nets to the right side." It was Jesus, but they didn't know it. They did what He said and pulled up so many fish that they could not lift the net.

Then John, the apostle, knew Who was on the shore. "It's the Lord," he shouted. Peter was so excited that he jumped into the water and swam to the beach.

There on the shore, a fire was built. Fish were being cooked. Jesus asked the apostles to eat. After they ate, Jesus asked Peter three times, "Do you love Me?"

Each time Peter said, "You know that I love you." Then Jesus said, "Feed my sheep. Feed my lambs." This meant that Jesus wanted Peter to take care of all His followers. Peter became the first Pope.

Soon the time came for Jesus to go back to His Heavenly Father. The apostles were sad that He was going. They did not feel ready to go and preach without Jesus at their side. But Jesus promised to send the Holy Spirit. He would show them what to do and make them strong enough to do it.

Jesus walked up a mountain with His friends. "Go and teach everyone. Baptize them in the name of the Father, and of the Son, and of the Holy Spirit. I will be with you always, even to the end of time."

Then Jesus rose up into the sky and went back to Heaven. There He is King of Heaven and earth. He has prepared a place in Heaven for all those who love Him. Someday, at the end of the world, Jesus will come again to judge the living and the dead.

"Go into the whole world and proclaim the Good News to all creation."　　(Mark 16:15)

Words to Know:

Ascension　　apostles

Q. 38 *What did Jesus Christ do after His Resurrection?*
After His Resurrection, Jesus Christ remained on earth for forty days and then He ascended to Heaven.

Being an Apostle of Jesus

"Let's take some candy from the store," Susan's friends say. "No one will see us do it."

"Not me," said Susan. "It's wrong to steal. It's a sin."

Jack and a few boys are on their way to Little League. Some of Jack's friends are not Catholic. They walk by the church and Jack sees the door is open.

"Hey, wait a minute. I want to go in and say a prayer. Come on in with me and I'll show you around my church."

These children know how to be apostles. They share the Good News about Jesus by showing others what is right.

How can you be an apostle to people you know?

30 The Coming of The Holy Spirit

After the Ascension the apostles stayed in a house with Mary. They prayed together for nine days. Then, all at once, the sound of a great wind filled the house. Little flames of fire came and rested on each of them.

The apostles were filled with the Holy Spirit. They were not afraid anymore. They left the house and began to teach about Jesus. The Holy Spirit had given them many gifts. One was that people from all over the world could understand what the apostles were saying. And the Holy Spirit helped them to preach so well that many people believed in Jesus. Three thousand people were baptized that day!

The Holy Spirit that came to the apostles is the Third Person of the Holy Trinity. The Holy Spirit came to us at Baptism. He helps us to pray and to love. He gives us the grace to win the fight against sin. He helps us understand the things we learn about God.

The day the Holy Spirit came to the apostles is called Pentecost Sunday. We celebrate this day in church each year. We also call Pentecost Sunday the "Birthday of the Church". Those who were baptized on Pentecost were the first members.

We have talked a lot this year about the Sacraments of Baptism, Penance, and the Holy Eucharist. A sacrament is a special gift from Jesus that gives us grace. Whenever a sacrament is received, special words and things are used as signs of the grace God gives us. There are seven sacraments in all:

1. Baptism: When original sin is washed away. We receive the new life of grace and become children of God.

2. Penance: When our sins are forgiven by Jesus through the priest.

3. Holy Eucharist: When we receive the Body and Blood of Jesus under the appearance of bread and wine.

4. Confirmation: When the Holy Spirit comes to us with His gifts, just as He did to the apostles at Pentecost. Grownups and older boys and girls receive this sacrament.

5. Marriage: When a man and woman marry each other they stand before the Church and make promises to live together according to God's laws, and to help each other grow holy.

6. Holy Orders: When a man receives this sacrament he becomes a priest. A bishop lays hands on the man's head and gives him the power to forgive sins and say Mass.

7. Anointing of the Sick: When someone is very sick or in danger of death, he can receive a blessing with holy oil. This will give him the grace to die in God's friendship, or it may even heal him of the sickness.

Words to Know:

Pentecost

Q. 39 *Who is the Holy Spirit?*
The Holy Spirit is the Third Person of the Holy Trinity.

We Pray:

Come Holy Spirit,
fill the hearts of your faithful
and enkindle in us the fire of Your Love.

125

31 God's Family—The Church

The apostles preached and baptized in many lands. The Church grew and grew. Today there are Christians in every part of the world.

Jesus made Peter the head of His Church on earth. Today the Pope has Peter's job. He is the leader of Catholics everywhere. Bishops carry on the work of the apostles. There are thousands of bishops in different parts of the world. They look after us as good shepherds taking care of their sheep. The bishops take the place of Jesus on earth.

The Pope and bishops with him teach us in Jesus' name. They explain the Bible to us and tell us how to lead good lives. They also make rules about the Mass and the sacraments. Everything Jesus wants us to know is taught by the Catholic Church.

Each bishop has many helpers called priests. Priests receive special powers from the bishop. They can forgive sins in the Sacrament of Penance. They can change bread and wine into the Body and Blood of Christ.

Some members of God's family live a special kind of life. They promise to spend all their time doing God's work. We call them Religious Sisters and Brothers. They teach, work in hospitals, help the poor, and spend the whole day praying for us all.

Most members of God's family are not bishops, priests, or sisters. They are men, women, boys, and girls like those you see each Sunday in church. Each of us has an important part to play in the Church.

The Church is like a body. A body has many parts. If even one small part is hurt or missing, the whole body suffers. Each small part does something that the others cannot do. That is how the Church is. You can help the Church in a way that no one else can. And the prayers and actions of many others help you.

The Church makes us holy. It brings the grace of God to everyone. Each of us can receive that grace and become holy. We can also bring God's grace and love to others.

Words to Know:

Pope   bishop   Church

Q. 40 *What is the Church?*
The Church is the family of all baptized people.

Q. 41 *Who founded the Church?*
Jesus Christ is the founder of the Church.

Q. 42 *Who is the Pope?*
The Pope is the head of the Church, who takes the place of Jesus on earth.

Everything we believe is in a prayer called the *Apostles' Creed*. The word "creed" means what we believe.

APOSTLES' CREED

I believe in God, the Father Almighty, Creator of Heaven and earth, and in Jesus Christ, His only Son, our Lord, Who was conceived by the Holy Spirit, born of the Virgin Mary, suffered under Pontius Pilate, was crucified, died, and was buried. He descended into Hell; the third day He rose again from the dead. He ascended into Heaven and sits at the right hand of God, the Father Almighty; from thence He shall come to judge the living and the dead. I believe in the Holy Spirit, the Holy Catholic Church, the Communion of Saints, the forgiveness of sins, the resurrection of the body, and life everlasting. *Amen.*

32   Mary Our Mother

Mary was with the apostles at Pentecost. During the days after Pentecost Mary did everything she could to help the new Church grow. She wanted everyone to know about what her Son had done for all men.

When it was time for Mary's life to end, God did something very special for her. He took her, body and soul, into Heaven. How happy Mary was to see her Son again! Jesus made His Mother the Queen of Heaven and earth.

Do you remember how Jesus gave His Mother to us when He was dying on the Cross? Mary is Mother of the Church and the Mother of each of us. We can pray to Mary and tell her about our problems. She will understand. We can learn from Mary how to be good. She always did what God wanted her to do and she never sinned. If you are ever tempted to do something wrong, ask Mary to help you.

Mary has a special love for little children. Sometimes she lets them see her. About seventy years ago she came down from Heaven to visit two girls and a boy who lived in Fatima, Portugal. She asked them to make sacrifices for sinners and to say the rosary every day. The children thought Mary was the most beautiful, wonderful person they had ever seen. They were happy to do what she said.

Today millions of people say the rosary each day for world peace, because of what Mary told those three children. She told them that we would only have peace if we were good and pleasing to God.

Queen of Angels
Queen of Apostles
Queen of all Saints   } *Pray for us*
Queen of the most holy Rosary
Queen of Peace

Words to Know:

rosary

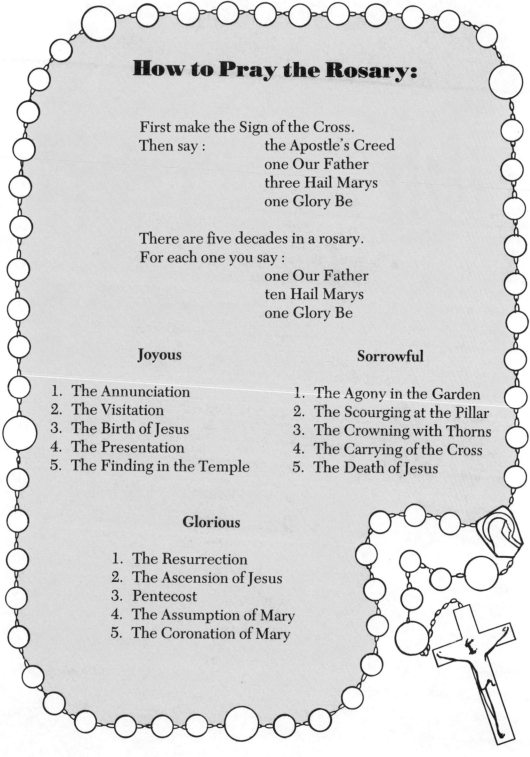

How to Pray the Rosary:

First make the Sign of the Cross.
Then say : the Apostle's Creed
one Our Father
three Hail Marys
one Glory Be

There are five decades in a rosary.
For each one you say :
one Our Father
ten Hail Marys
one Glory Be

Joyous

1. The Annunciation
2. The Visitation
3. The Birth of Jesus
4. The Presentation
5. The Finding in the Temple

Sorrowful

1. The Agony in the Garden
2. The Scourging at the Pillar
3. The Crowning with Thorns
4. The Carrying of the Cross
5. The Death of Jesus

Glorious

1. The Resurrection
2. The Ascension of Jesus
3. Pentecost
4. The Assumption of Mary
5. The Coronation of Mary

33 Jesus Is Always Present

Before He ascended into Heaven, Jesus said, "I am with you always, even to the end of time."

Jesus is with us in many ways. He sent us His Spirit to lead and guide us. He is with His Church. He teaches us through our Holy Father, the Pope.

But Jesus is with us in a special way through the Holy Eucharist. At the Consecration, Jesus comes to us under the appearance of bread and wine. After Mass, some of the Consecrated Hosts are put in the tabernacle. You can tell that Jesus is present in the tabernacle when a special lamp, called the sanctuary lamp, is lit. So Jesus lives in every Catholic church in the world. He is there as really and truly as He was in Bethlehem.

Since Jesus gave us so great a gift, we should receive Him whenever we can in Holy Communion. Most churches offer Mass every day of the week. Maybe you can find a way to go more often.

We can visit the church during the week. Jesus is there in the tabernacle. He would love to have you come and talk to Him for a little while. Visits to church are one way to receive much grace. You will be happier and holier after you make these visits. If the church door is locked, say hello to Jesus, and a short prayer, before you go. He will hear you and be very pleased.

Sometimes your church may have a special time of worship that is not the Mass. It may be a holy hour or a benediction. The priest takes the Host from the tabernacle. He places it in a monstrance. Then everyone can see and adore Jesus in the Holy Eucharist. The priest blesses the people and they sing a special song or say special prayers.

In church, we must act like big boys and girls who know that Jesus is really there. Babies make noise and run in church because they do not know about Jesus. But those who know and love Him do not talk in church. We walk quietly to our seats. We genuflect with respect. We do not turn around and stare at others. We spend our time in loving prayer with Jesus.

Monstrance: A beautiful holder for the Host. It is used at benediction services.

We Pray:

THE DIVINE PRAISES

Blessed be God.
Blessed be His Holy Name.
Blessed be Jesus Christ, true God and true Man.
Blessed be the Name of Jesus.
Blessed be His Most Sacred Heart.
Blessed be His Most Precious Blood.
Blessed be Jesus in the Most Holy Sacrament of the Altar.
Blessed be the Holy Spirit, the Paraclete.
Blessed be the great Mother of God, Mary most holy.
Blessed be her holy and Immaculate Conception.
Blessed be her glorious Assumption.
Blessed be the name of Mary, Virgin and Mother.
Blessed be St. Joseph, her most chaste spouse.
Blessed be God in His angels and in His saints.

Sanctuary Lamp: A special light that always burns by the tabernacle to let us know that Jesus is there.

Tabernacle: A boxlike container in our churches where the Holy Eucharist is kept.

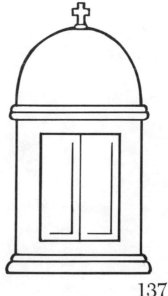

137

34   Heaven, Our Home

We all die someday. Our souls leave our bodies. If we have loved God in this life, we will be ready to love God forever. God will welcome us into Heaven. We will be happy there forever. We will see Jesus and Mary and people in our family who have died. The souls in Heaven are called saints.

Some will die with their souls almost ready for God, but not quite. Maybe there are venial sins they are not sorry for. Before these souls go to Heaven, they go for a while to Purgatory to be made clean of all sin. Souls in Purgatory are sad because they do not see God, but happy because they know that they will see Him soon.

If a person has not loved God in this life and dies with a mortal sin on his soul, he will not be able to love God or want to be with Him. A soul that hates God will be in a place called Hell.

At the end of the world our souls will be reunited with our bodies. We will be able to enjoy Heaven with both our bodies and souls.

That is why it is important to live according to God's laws. Each good thing we do makes us pleasing to God and ready for Heaven. Even little things like saying our prayers and cheerfully helping others help to get us ready.

Heaven is our real home. Earth is only a place where we stay for awhile and learn to love God. Jesus told us to spend our life "storing up treasure in Heaven". We can begin right now. The sight of the Blessed Trinity and the Mother of God will be more beautiful than anything we know. Let's pray every day for God to make us saints!

Words to Know:

Hell   Purgatory   saints

Words to Know

Abraham: The father of God's chosen people, the Jews.

Absolution: The words said by the priest in the Sacrament of Penance that take away our sins.

Adam and Eve: The first man and woman God made. We call them our first parents because everyone came from them.

Advent: The four weeks before Christmas when we get ready for the birth of Jesus.

Angels: Spirits made by God. Angels are God's helpers.

Apostles: The twelve friends of Jesus who went out to tell others about Jesus after the Ascension. They became the first bishops.

Ascension: When Jesus went back to Heaven forty days after Easter.

Baptism: The sacrament which takes away original sin. It gives us the new life of grace and makes us children of God.

Benediction: A church service that honors Jesus in the Holy Eucharist.

Bethlehem: The town where Jesus was born.

Bible: The holy book that God gave us. It tells us about God, His chosen people, the Savior He sent, and the early days of the Church.

Bishop: A man who does the work of the apostles and takes care of a large group of Catholics.

Calvary: The hilltop where Jesus died.

Christmas: The birthday of Jesus.

Church: The group of followers of Jesus who believe the same faith, receive the sacraments, and obey the Pope. Another name for the family of God.

Communion: See *Holy Eucharist*.

Confession: Another name for the Sacrament of Penance. It is the part of the Sacrament where we tell our sins to the priest.

Consecration: The part of the Mass when the priest changes the bread and wine into the Body and Blood of Jesus.

Creator: God is our Creator. That means He made us and all things.

Creed: The part of the Mass where we stand and say how we believe in God.

David: The boy who killed Goliath and grew up to be king. Jesus was descended from the family of David.

Devils: Bad angels who went against God.

Disciple: A follower of Jesus.

Easter: The day we celebrate the Resurrection of Jesus.

Fasting: Eating no food or less food as a way to do penance.

Forgiveness: The act of pardoning someone who has done something wrong.

Gabriel: The angel who came to Mary and told her she would be the Mother of Jesus.

Genuflection: A sign of reverence we make when we are in front of the tabernacle. We genuflect by kneeling on the right knee and getting up again.

Good News: What Jesus came to tell us and do for us.

Good Shepherd: A name for Jesus, because He takes care of us the way a shepherd cares for his sheep.

Good Samaritan: Someone who helps others who are in need.

Grace: The life of God in our souls. We receive grace from the sacraments, from prayer, and from doing good.

Guardian Angel: A special angel given to each of us by God to help us.

Heaven: The place of reward for those who were good and asked God to forgive their sins. In Heaven we see God and are happy with Him forever.

Hell: The place where someone goes that has turned away from God in mortal sin and would not be sorry for that sin.

Holy Eucharist: The sacrament in which Jesus comes to us in the form of bread and wine; the Body and Blood of Jesus.

Holy Family: Jesus, Mary, and Joseph.

Isaac: The son of Abraham.

John the Baptist: The cousin of Jesus. John was the last of the prophets. He prepared people for the coming of Jesus.

Joseph: The foster-father of Jesus and husband of Mary.

Kingdom of God: In this world, God's Kingdom is His Church; in the next world, it is Heaven.

Last Supper: The dinner Jesus had with the apostles the night before He died. At the Last Supper Jesus gave us the Holy Eucharist.

Law: A rule that tells us how to act.

Manger: The wooden box used to feed animals. Mary used a manger for baby Jesus' bed.

Mary: The Mother of Jesus. Mary is Mother of the Church and our Mother, too.

Mass: The sacrifice of Jesus on the Cross offered by the priest in our church.

Miracle: Something wonderful that is done by the power of God and that only God can do.

Monstrance: A beautiful holder for the Host. It is used at a benediction service.

Morning Offering: A prayer we say each day. It offers all we will do and think and say to God.

Mortal Sin: A very big sin that kills all life of grace in a soul.

Moses: A leader of the Jewish people to whom God gave the Ten Commandments.

Mystery: Something that we cannot understand, but we believe because God has told us it is true.

Nazareth: The town where Jesus lived with Mary and Joseph.

Noah: The good man that built the ark to save his family and the animals from the great flood.

To Obey: To do what we are told. We should obey God's laws.

To Offend: Sin offends God. That means sin makes God sad.

Offertory: The part of the Mass where bread and wine are brought to the altar to become the Body and Blood of Jesus.

Original Sin: The first sin committed when Adam and Eve disobeyed God. We are all born with original sin on our souls.

Passion: The sufferings of Jesus.

Penance: The sacrament in which all sins committed after Baptism are forgiven. It is also a prayer we say or something we do to make up for our sins.

Pentecost: The coming of the Holy Spirit to the apostles.

Praise: The kind of prayer or song that tells God how great and good He is.

Priest: A man who has received the sacrament of Holy Orders and who can forgive our sins and say Mass.

Prophets: Those who prepared the people for the coming of the Savior.

Purgatory: The place where a soul may go to be made clean from all sin before it can go to Heaven.

Resurrection: When Jesus rose from the dead.

Rosary: A special prayer honoring Mary, the Mother of God.

Sacrament: A sign given by Jesus that brings us grace.

Sacrifice: Something that is offered to God. At Mass we offer Jesus to the Father as a sacrifice for our sins.

Saint: A holy person who loved God very much on earth and now is in Heaven.

Sanctuary Lamp: A special light that always burns by the tabernacle to let us know that Jesus is there.

To Serve: To do what God wants us to do. To do God's work.

Sin: Any wrong that we do. Sin turns us away from God.

Soul: The part of us that thinks, loves, and wishes good or evil. The soul lives forever.

Tabernacle: The special place in our church where the Holy Eucharist is kept.

Ten Commandments: The laws given by God to Moses.

Trinity: The mystery that tells us God is three divine Persons in one God.

Venial Sin: A small sin that makes a soul less pleasing to God.

We Pray

THE SIGN OF THE CROSS

In the Name of the Father, and of the Son, and of the Holy Spirit. *Amen*.

GLORY BE

Glory be to the Father, and to the Son, and to the Holy Spirit, as it was in the beginning, is now, and ever shall be, world without end. *Amen*.

HAIL MARY

Hail Mary, full of grace! The Lord is with thee. Blessed art thou among women, and blessed is the fruit of thy womb, Jesus.
Holy Mary, Mother of God, pray for us sinners, now and at the hour of our death. *Amen*.

MORNING OFFERING

O my God, I offer You every thought and word and act of today. Please bless me, my God, and make me good today. *Amen*.

OUR FATHER

Our Father, Who art in Heaven, hallowed be Thy Name; Thy Kingdom come; Thy will be done on earth as it is in Heaven. Give us this day our daily bread, and forgive us our trespasses as we forgive those who trespass against us; and lead us not into temptation, but deliver us from evil. *Amen*.

ACT OF CONTRITION

O my God, I am heartily sorry for having offended You. I detest all my sins because of Your just punishments, but most of all because they offend You, my God, Who are all-good and deserving of all my love. I firmly resolve, with the help of Your grace, to confess my sins, to do penance, and to amend my life. *Amen*.

PRAYER TO THE GUARDIAN ANGEL

Angel of God, my guardian dear,
To whom God's love commits me here,
Ever this day be at my side,
To light and guard, to rule and guide. *Amen*.

APOSTLES' CREED

I believe in God, the Father Almighty, Creator of Heaven and earth, and in Jesus Christ, His only Son, our Lord, Who was conceived by the Holy Spirit, born of the Virgin Mary, suffered under Pontius Pilate, was crucified, died, and was buried. He descended into Hell; the third day He rose again from the dead. He ascended into Heaven and sits at the right hand of God, the Father Almighty; from thence He shall come to judge the living and the dead. I believe in the Holy Spirit, the Holy Catholic Church, the Communion of Saints, the forgiveness of sins, the resurrection of the body, and life everlasting. *Amen.*